Measurement

by

Karen Bryant-Mole

Illustrated by

John Yates

Notes for teachers and parents

This book investigates the measurement of length, mass (weight), capacity, area and volume. In length the units centimetre, metre and kilometre are introduced; in mass, kilogram and gram; in capacity, litre, centilitre and millilitre; in area, square centimetres and square metres and in volume, cubic centimetres and cubic metres. The book also helps children choose the most appropriate unit of measurement for particular measuring activities.

Understanding Maths

Adding and Subtracting
Numbers
Measurement
Shape
Graphs and Charts
Multiplying and Dividing

Series editor: Deborah Elliott
Edited by Zoë Hargreaves
Designed by Malcolm Walker
Commissioned photography by Zul Mukhida

First published in 1992 by
Wayland (Publishers) Limited
61 Western Road, Hove,
East Sussex BN3 1JD

British Library Cataloguing in Publication Data
Bryant-Mole, Karen
    Measuring - (Understanding maths)
    I. Title II. Series
    372.7

    ISBN 0 7502 0012 X

Phototypeset by Malcolm Walker
Printed by G. Canale & C.S.p.A., Turin
Bound by Casterman S.A., Belgium

Contents

Centimetres

Leila is brushing her teeth before going to bed.
Can you see the yellow toothbrush in the cup next to the curtain?

How wide do you think the toothbrush is across the top?

When someone asks you how wide, how long or how tall something is you could compare it with another object and say 'It's about as wide as a ...'

Do you think the top of the toothbrush is about the same width as an ice-lolly stick or a birthday card?

You could use several tiny objects to measure it. For example, you could say the top of the toothbrush is about four grains of rice wide.

These answers don't really say exactly how wide the toothbrush is because we don't know how wide the grains of rice are or how wide the lollystick is.

To measure something exactly you need to use units that always mean the same length. To measure something small, like this toothbrush, you would use centimetres.

One lolly stick might be thin and another might be fat, but there is no such thing as a fat centimetre or a thin centimetre.

A centimetre is always the same.

—

This line is one centimetre long. The short way of writing centimetre is **cm**.

The yellow toothbrush in the photograph looks as if it might be about 1 cm wide. To find out exactly how wide it is we need to measure it. To measure it we need to use a ruler.

Rulers are marked out in centimetres. There are three different types of ruler. This is where you start to measure with each of them.

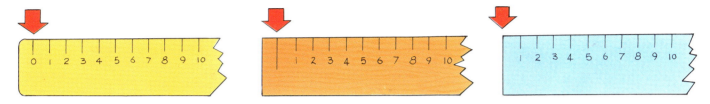

Leila decides to find out exactly how long her green toothbrush is. How long is Leila's toothbrush?

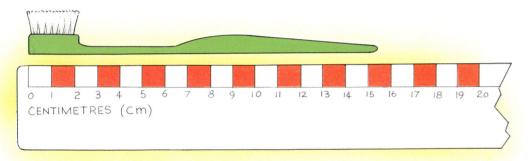

Look at the other end of the toothbrush and see which number it is nearest to. It is between the 15 and the 16 but is nearer to the 15. So, Leila's toothbrush is about 15 cm long.

Find a ruler and measure these objects.

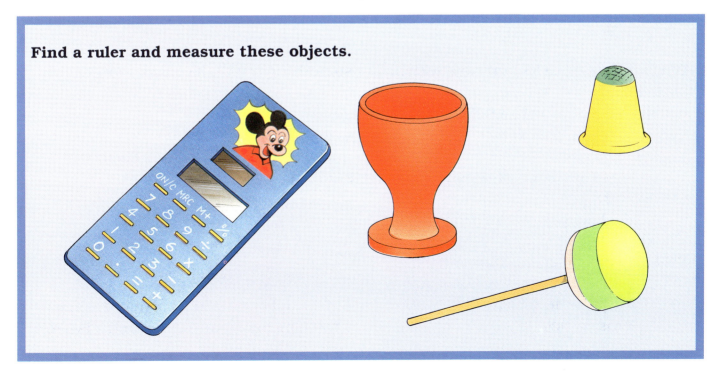

Metres

Lawrence is playing in the snow. Lawrence is exactly 100 cm tall. The word 'centimetre' means 'hundredth of a metre'. 100 'hundredths of a metre' is the same as 1 metre. The short way of writing metre is **m**.

1 m is about the height of most four-year-old children.

1 m is about the length of an adult's stride.

1 m is about the height of an average kitchen unit.

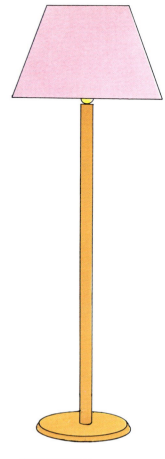

Look around your home for some large objects. Decide whether they measure more than 1 m, less than 1 m or about 1 m.

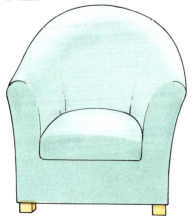

Sometimes measuring things in whole metres is just not accurate enough. This window is about 1 m high. It is longer than 1 m but it is nearer to 1 m than 2 m.
What would happen if you bought curtains for this window that were 1 m long?
Would they fit?

In order to buy curtains that fit, you need to know exactly how long the window is.

When the length of the window was measured in centimetres it was found to be 135 cm. Instead of describing the length of the window in centimetres it can be written as metres and parts of a metre.
135 cm is made up of 100 cm (which we know is 1 whole metre) and 35 cm (which we know is 35 'hundredths of a

metre'). Hundredths can be written as parts of a whole number using decimals. 135 cm can be written as 1·35 m.

Look at the labels in these clothes. They tell you the height of person they are designed to fit. The heights are written in centimetres. Can you describe them in metres?

Kilometres

Long distances, like the distances aeroplanes travel, are measured in kilometres. The 'kilo' part of the word kilometre means 'thousand'. A kilometre is the same distance as 1000 m.
The short way of writing kilometre is **km**.

Planes travel many thousands of kilometres. You could easily walk 1 km. It would probably take you about twelve minutes to walk 1 km. Think of some of the distances you walk and how long they take. The walk from home to school, perhaps, or the walk to the nearest shop. Do you think they are more than, less than or about 1 km?

Here are some different ways of travelling.

Which would be the most suitable for travelling 1 km? Which would you use to travel 100 km and which would you use to travel 10 000 km?

The speed something travels at is described as a particular number of kilometres per hour. If you walk at a speed of 1 km every 12 minutes you are walking at 5 km per hour, because there are 5 sets of 12 minutes in every 60 minutes or hour.

Look again at the vehicles.
One can travel at 1920 km per hour, one at 110 km per hour and one at 15 km per hour.
Which vehicle travels at which speed?

If you know how fast something travels and you know how long a journey takes, you can work out how far it has travelled.

If a car is driven at 80 km per hour and travels for an hour it will have covered 80 km. If it travels for half an hour it will have covered half that distance, which is 40 km
(80 km ÷ 2 = 40 km).
If it travels for a quarter of an hour it will only have covered a quarter of that distance, or 20 km
(80 km ÷ 4 = 20 km).

Mrs Ansty's Journey

Mrs Ansty is visiting her sister. She has a complicated journey. First of all she rides her bicycle to the station. Then she catches a train and finally gets a taxi to her sister's house. She rides her bicycle for half an hour, travelling at 14 km per hour. The train takes one hour, travelling at 102 km per hour. The taxi takes a quarter of an hour at 60 km per hour.

How many kilometres is her journey?

Drawing to scale

Jenny is a surveyor. She is looking at the plans of a house which is being built. When plans are drawn up they have to be made very accurately.

The bricklayers need to know exactly how long to build the walls.

The carpenters need to know exactly what size the window frames should be.

The plumbers need to know exactly where the water pipes should go.

So when the plans are drawn up they are drawn 'to scale'. When something is drawn to scale it is an exact picture of the real thing only smaller.

Look at Dawn's kitchen. It is 9 m long and 6 m wide.

Now look at this scale drawing of the kitchen. It is marked out on squared paper. Every square is 1 cm long and 1 cm wide. The drawing of the kitchen is 9 cm long and 6 cm wide. Every metre of real kitchen has been drawn as 1 cm.

Scale drawings are also used to show bigger measurements.

Maps and atlases are good examples of scale drawings.

Every scale drawing will tell you exactly what scale it has been drawn to.

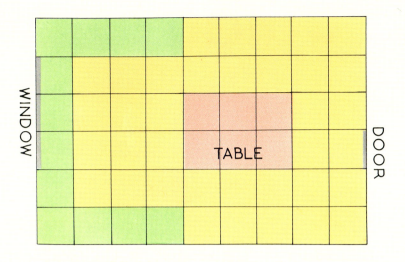

Dawn's parents wish to replace the old cupboards in their kitchen with some new ones. They have used the scale drawing to plan a new layout for their kitchen.
Each new unit will be 1 m wide.
Every unit is shaded green.
How many of the new units must they buy?

The rest of the plan is also drawn to scale.
Can you work out how wide the window is?
How wide is the door?
How long is the table?

See if you can make a scale drawing of your bedroom.

A map of your town might be drawn on a scale of 5 cm for every kilometre. A map of the USA might be drawn on a scale of 5 cm for every 1000 km.

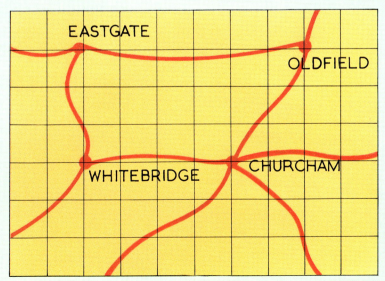

Look at this map which is drawn on a scale of 1 cm to 1 km. It is marked out in centimetre squares.

How far is it from Whitebridge to Churcham?
Which is the shortest route from Whitebridge to Oldfield?
Is it more or less than 5 km from Whitebridge to Eastgate?

Kilograms

Length, height and distance are all measured in centimetres, metres or kilometres.
How do you find out how heavy something is?
You can't measure that with a ruler! You have to use another set of measuring units.

Most of the produce on this stall is sold in 'kilograms'.

These apples weigh about 1 kg. (**kg** is the short way of writing kilogram.)

Find a bag of sugar that weighs 1 kg.
Feel how heavy it is and then look at these photographs.

Which shows something weighing more than 1 kg, less than 1 kg and about 1 kg?

We can use kilograms to find out how much we weigh.

If you look at this set of weighing scales you can see that the red marker is on 0 kg. In the same way that it was very important to start measuring with the ruler at 0 cm, in weighing you must make sure that the indicator is on 0 kg. If it is not you will not get an accurate reading.

To find out how much you weigh, stand on the scales and read the number indicated by the red marker.

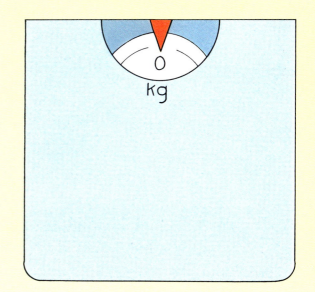

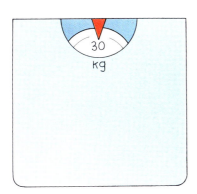
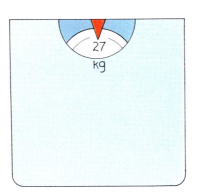
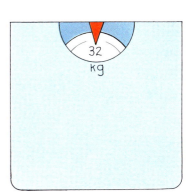

Chris, Ahmed, Joe and Sarah have all weighed themselves. These scales show how much they weigh. Look at each one and read the weight.

Sarah is lighter than Joe but heavier than Chris. Ahmed is heavier than Sarah, Joe and Chris.

Can you use this information to work out how much each child weighs?

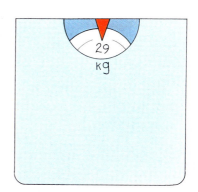

13

Grams

We have already discovered that the 'kilo' in kilometre means one thousand. The same is true of the word 'kilogram'. A kilogram is made up of 1000 grams.

Grams are very useful when weighing light objects. A gram is the weight of about two envelopes.

The sweet seller in the picture above usually sells his sweets in grams.

This is what 100 gm of sweets look like. (**gm** is the short way of writing grams.)

Make your own weighing machine and weights

You will need:

**a wire coat hanger
a cotton reel
two identical large
 yoghurt pots
a circle of card
sticky tape
thin string
plasticine
100 gm chocolate
 bar**

Tie the cotton reel to one end of a piece of string. Attach the other end to the coat hanger as shown. Fold the circle of card in half and hang it over the bottom rail. Draw a line down the centre of the card. Make a handle for each yoghurt pot using equal lengths of string. Loop one over each end of the hanger. Allow the hanger to swing freely. The cotton reel and string should hang directly down the line on the card. If not, stick a little plasticine round the wire on the lighter side until the two sides balance.

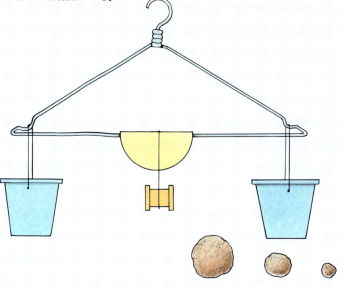

How to make the weights

Find something with the weight already printed on it, such as 100 gm bar of chocolate. Put the chocolate into one of the pots and a ball of plasticine into the other. Balance the two pots by adding more plasticine or taking some away. Now you have a 100 gm ball of plasticine. Get another lump of plasticine and make another 100 gm ball. Break it into two equal pieces. Balance these pieces. Now you have two 50 gm balls. Take one of the 50 gm balls and break it into two equal pieces. Balance them and you have two 25 gm pieces.

Use your set of weights to find how much small objects weigh. You will not be able to get a completely accurate measurement but you will be able to find out roughly how much they weigh.

This book weighs 1500 gm.

We can describe this in kilograms using decimals.

1500 gm is the same as 1 whole kilogram (1000 gm) and 500 thousandths of a kilogram (500 gm).
Write the whole kilogram first, '1', and then put in the decimal point and the 500 thousandths, '1·500 kg'.
In decimals, unlike whole numbers, you can get rid of any spare 0s at the end of the number.
So, 1500 gm is the same as 1·5 kg.

Litres

Pierre and Christophe are picking grapes. The grapes will be used to make wine. The wine is stored in large barrels and is then put into bottles before being sold.

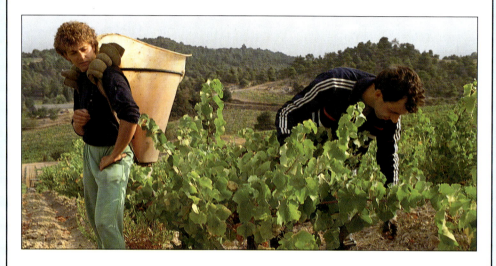

How much does this bottle hold?

If we wanted to measure the height of the bottle we would use centimetres.
If we wanted to measure the weight of the bottle we would use grams.
But if we want to measure the amount of liquid the bottle holds (its capacity) we have to use litres.
This bottle holds exactly 1 litre. The short way of writing litre is **l**.

The amount a bottle holds can be hard to estimate. Look at these bottles and guess which holds 1 litre, which holds more and which holds less. It may not seem possible but all of these containers hold exactly the same amount of liquid. They are all 1 litre containers. Collect lots of empty 1 litre containers like these and try filling one with water and then tipping the contents from one to another.

Make this delicious drink for your friends.

You will need:

1 l lemonade
1 l grapefruit juice
2 lemons
ice-cubes
drinking straws

Not all containers hold 1 litre. Some are measured in centilitres. The word 'centilitre' means 'hundredth of a litre'. There are 100 cl in a litre. (**cl** is the short way of writing centilitre).

Fruit Cooler

1. Pour the lemonade and grapefruit juice into a large bowl (or any other container that will hold at least 2 l) and stir very gently.
2. Cut one of the lemons in half and squeeze the juice from both halves into the mixture in the bowl.
3. Find some glasses and put two or three ice-cubes in each glass.
4. Use a ladle to pour the drink into the glasses.
5. Place a slice of lemon and a straw in each glass.

Now you have a delicious drink.

Millilitres

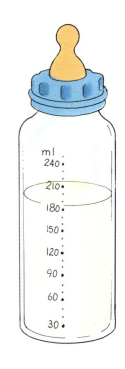

Here is a baby's bottle. It is marked out in millilitres.

Laura is six weeks old. She is being fed some milk. Laura's mum makes up her feed by putting a number of scoops of powdered milk into an exact amount of water.

Litres and centilitres are not exact enough to measure the amount of water needed for Laura's feed.

A measurement that is even more precise is needed. So Laura's mum uses millilitres. A millilitre is one thousandth of a litre. The short way of writing millilitre is **ml**.

The amount of milk a baby needs depends on his or her weight.

This chart shows the average weight of a baby and how many scoops of powdered milk and millilitres of water are needed to make up each feed.

How many millilitres of water should be added to the milk for a three-month-old baby?
How many should be added for a five-month-old baby?
If Laura is six weeks old, how many millilitres of water should be added to her powdered milk?

AGE	WEIGHT kg	NUMBER OF FEEDS	SCOOPS	WATER ml
0–2 WKS	3·5	6		
3–6 WKS	4	5	3	90
2 MTHS	5	5	4	120
3 MTHS	6	5	5	150
4 MTHS	6·5	5	6	180
5 MTHS	7	5	6	180
6 MTHS	7·5	4	6	180
7–9 MTHS	8·5	3	7	210
10–12 MTHS	9	2	7	210
			7	210

These spoons are sometimes used to measure in millilitres.

A large teaspoon or medicine spoon holds 5 ml.
A dessert spoon holds 10 ml.
A tablespoon holds 15 ml.

Here are parts of three recipes.
What sort of spoon would you use in each?

250 gm BUTTER

5 ml SALT

15 ml HONEY

100 gm OATS

10 ml MILK

50 gm SUGAR

Area

Suki has her pink shoes on today. How would we measure one of her shoes?

We could measure how wide it is and how long it is. We can also measure the amount of ground her shoe covers. This is called the 'area' of her shoe.

The easiest way to find the area of something like a shoe is to draw around the shoe on a piece of paper. Suki has drawn around her shoe on a piece of paper that is marked out in squares 1 cm long and 1 cm wide. Each square is called a 'square centimetre'.

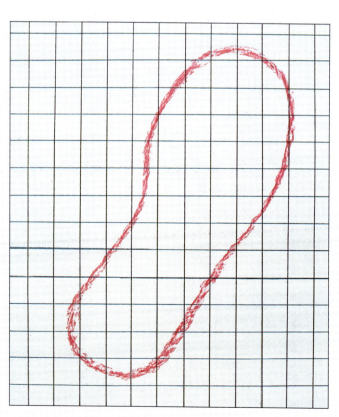

To find out the rough area of her shoe Suki has to count the number of square centimetres inside the outline of her shoe.

There are 38 complete squares, so Suki could say that the area of her shoe is about 38 square centimetres. If Suki wanted to make the calculation even more accurate she could look at the partly shaded squares too. She could count up the number of squares that are more than half shaded but ignore the squares that are less than half shaded.

Using this method Suki thinks her shoe has an area of about 48 square centimetres.

Do you agree?

Friendly feet

Rikki loves to sleep in his pram with his foot hanging over the edge! Whose foot do you think has the larger area, Suki's or Rikki's?

Here is the outline of Rikki's foot drawn on paper marked out in square centimetres. Estimate the area of his foot as accurately as possible.

Which of these is near to or the same as your estimate?

12   square centimetres.
19   square centimetres.
 4   square centimetres.

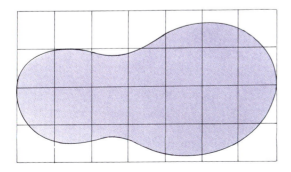

Find some paper marked out in square centimetres (graph paper will do) or make some yourself using a ruler.

Give some friends a sheet each and ask them to place one foot on the paper and draw around their shoes.

Find the area of each person's shoe and put them in a row in order of size.

Now measure the length of each shoe from the tip of the toe to the heel. Put them in order of length.

Does the foot with the greatest area have to be the longest foot?

Will the order of feet according to area always be the same as the order according to length?

Why might the order be different?

Square metres

Mark is redecorating the dining room. In order to work out how much paint he had to buy he needed to know the area of the walls. If you look at the information on the side of a tin of paint you will probably find a section called 'coverage'. The manufacturers find out how many square metres of wall you can paint with every litre of paint, so that you can work out how much paint you need to buy. Before Mark decided how much paint to buy he needed to estimate the area of the walls.

A square metre is a square area 1 m high and 1 m long. Mark could have drawn lots of square metres all over his wall and counted up the number of squares. Counting squares is a good way of working out the area of things that are an irregular shape. For example, shapes with curves or shapes that are wide at one end and narrow at the other. There is a much easier way to work out the area of rectangles (shapes like walls or doors).

Look at this scale drawing of one of the dining room walls. It has been drawn on paper marked out in square centimetres.

In this drawing 1 cm represents 1 m and 1 square centimetre is the same as 1 square metre.

Rather than cover his walls in drawings of square metres, Mark can work out the area simply by measuring the height and length of each wall and multiplying the two numbers together.

What about the window and the door? Mark won't be painting the window and he will need to use a different type of paint on the door.

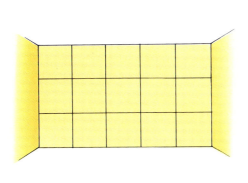

Count up the number of square centimetres.
There are 15.
The wall has a real area of 15 square metres.
Now use the drawing to work out how high the
wall of the room is and how long.
You should find that it is 3 m high and 5 m long.
3 x 5 = 15, which is the same number you arrived
at when you counted up the number of squares.

**The easiest way to work
out the area of the walls,
but not the window and
door, is to pretend that
they are not there and
that all the walls are
made completely out of
brick. Then you can work
out the areas of each
window and door and
take those areas away
from the total area.**

**It works like this.
This wall is drawn to the
same scale as the plan
above.**

**Count up the number of
square centimetres of
wall. Don't include the
window and door.
There are 12, which
represents 12 square
metres.**

**Now try it the other
way.
Multiply the height
and length of the wall,
which gives you
15 square metres.**

**Find the area of the
door.
You can see from the
plan that it must be
2 m high and 1 m
wide. 2 x 1 = 2, so the
door has an area of
2 square metres.
The window is 1 m
high and 1 m wide.
1 x 1 = 1, so the
window has an area of
1 square metre.
Take the area of the
door away from the
total area (15 - 2 = 13)
and then take away
the area of the window
(13 - 1 = 12).**

**The total area of wall
to be painted is,
therefore, 12 square
metres, which is
exactly the same
answer we had when
we counted up the
squares.**

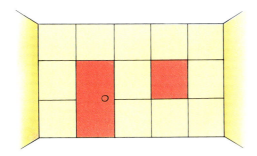

Volume

We have already discovered that the amount of flat space something covers is called its area, but that doesn't tell us how much space an object takes up altogether.

Look at this box.
We could draw around the bottom of the box and work out the area of the base. But that wouldn't tell us how much space the box takes up altogether. The box is three-dimensional (3-D). You can measure its height, length and depth. It does not just take up a flat amount of space, it takes up a 3-D amount of space.

The 3-D amount of space that something measures is called its volume.

This box is full of sugar cubes.

We found that we could measure area by counting up the number of squares a shape covered. We can measure volume in the same way by counting up the number of cubes that make up a shape.
A square is a 2-D shape with all its edges the same length.
A cube is a 3-D shape with all its edges the same length.

Squares are used in the measurement of 2-D shapes but cubes are used in the measurement of 3-D shapes.

Here are the cubes that were in the box.

They are arranged in exactly the same way as they were in the box.

There were 126 sugar cubes in this box.

Any shape you make out of the same number of cubes will have the same volume.
Here are some more ways of arranging the cubes.

All of these shapes have exactly the same volume because they are all made from the same number of cubes.

Find twelve cube-shaped bricks.

Can you make four different shapes with twelve bricks?

What is the tallest shape you can make?

What is the longest?

Cubic metres

Tom is repairing his driveway and he needs to buy some gravel.
Small amounts of gravel are usually sold by weight but this is not practical for large amounts. Large amounts of gravel are sold by volume.

We have already found out that volume can be measured using cubes but there has to be a standard cube that always stays the same.

Area is measured in square metres. A square metre is a square that is 1m high and 1m long.

Volume is measured in cubic metres.
A cubic metre is a cube that is 1 m high, 1 m long and 1 m deep.

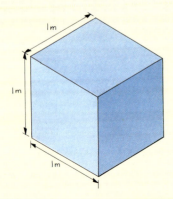

Volume is not just used to measure solid shapes.

You could measure the volume of a garage or a warehouse.
Look at this caravan and then look at the scale drawing of it.

In the drawing 1 cm represents 1 m.
The cubic metres are shown as cubes which are 1 cm high, 1 cm long and 1 cm deep.

How many cubes are there in each layer?
How many layers are there?
How many cubes are there altogether?

Look at the gravel in the picture.
It doesn't look like a cube does it?

Do you remember the sugar cubes?
The same number of cubes always had the same volume no matter how they were arranged.
The same is true with gravel. 1 cubic metre of gravel has the same volume whether it is packed in a cube shape or tipped into a heap.

In the same way that you can work out the area of a wall without drawing square metres all over it, you can work out the volume of the caravan without filling it with cubes.

Find out how many cubes there are in each layer by multiplying the number of cubes deep it is by the number of cubes long (6 x 3 = 18.)

If you multiply the number of cubes in each layer by the number of layers, 18 x 3 = 54, you reach the same number you first had when you counted up the cubes in the drawing. The volume of the caravan is 54 cubic metres.

So, to work out the volume of something you multiply the depth by the length and then multiply that answer by the height.

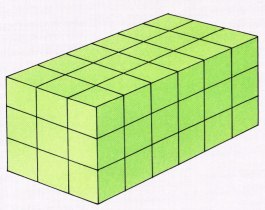

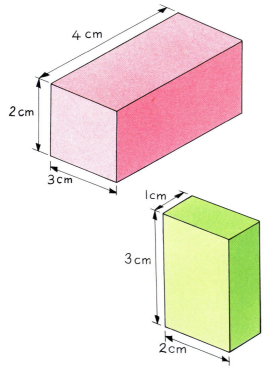

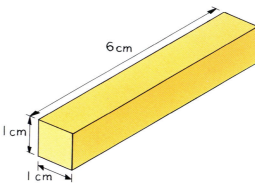

You can measure the volume of small things in cubic centimetres.
A cubic centimetre is a cube 1 cm high, 1 cm long and 1 cm deep.
Work out the volume of these boxes.

Which measurement?

Before you can measure something, you have to know what it is you want to measure. Do you want to measure its length, weight, capacity, area or volume?

Each of these types of measurement has its own set of measuring units.

Length is measured in centimetres, metres or kilometres.

Weight is measured in grams or kilograms.

Capacity is measured in millilitres, centilitres, or litres.

Area is measured in square centimetres or square metres.

Volume is measured in cubic centimetres or cubic metres.

Look at the toy box above.
Which type of measurement tells you the amount of liquid the toy box could hold?
Which would tell you the width of the toy box?
Which would tell you the size of the toy box's lid?
Which would tell you how heavy the toy box is?
Which would tell you how much space the toy box takes up?

Which of these objects would you use to measure:

the amount of juice in a cup?

the height of a flower?

the weight of a toy car?

the length of a worm?

the amount of milk in a carton?

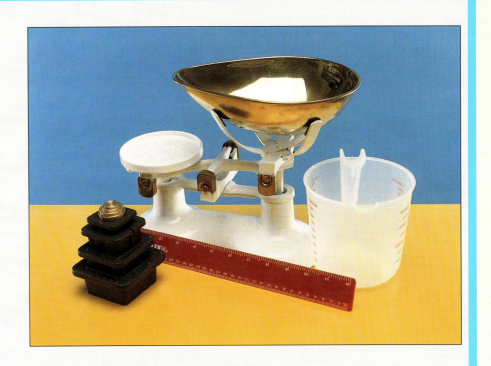

Area or Volume?

Would you use square centimetres or cubic centimetres to measure:
a page in a book?
a video tape?
a box of tissues?
a tissue?
a birthday card?
a lunch box?

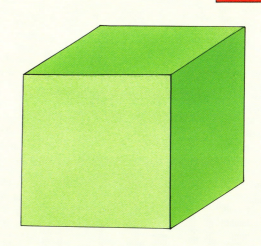

Glossary

area

the amount of flat space that something covers

atlas

a book of maps

centimetre

a hundredth part of a metre

estimate

to guess the size, quantity or value of something

gram

a very small weight. A thousandth part of a kilogram

kilogram

a measure of weight equal to 1000 grams

kilometre

a measure of length equal to 1000 metres

litre

a measure of capacity

metre

a measure of length equal to 100 centimetres

millilitre

a very small measure of capacity. A thousandth part of a litre

volume

the amount of space taken up by something

Books to read

Getting on with Measuring,
  Michael Holt, (Collins Educational)

Headstart: Measuring and Shape,
  Shirley Clarke (Headway, 1991)

Mastering Measurement,
  P. Toms (Hodder Educational, 1988)

Measuring,
  Michael Holt (Harper Collins, 1986)

Measuring,
  Latshmi Hewavisenti (Gloucester Press, 1991)

Photographs in this book were supplied by the following:

Chapel Studios   4, 6, 8, 9, 10, 11, 12, 14, 16, 20, 21, 26;
Eye Ubiquitous   7, 18, 22, 27;
Wayland Library   8, 9.

The Publisher wishes to thank all those individuals, particularly the children, who participated in and helped with the commissioned photography for this book.

Index